PIANO • VOCAL • GUITAR

FAVORITE·SONGS·FROM·JIM·HENSON'S
MUPPETS™

Contents

ISBN 978-0-7935-1830-2

HAL•LEONARD®
CORPORATION
7777 W. BLUEMOUND RD. P.O. BOX 13819 MILWAUKEE, WI 53213

Visit Hal Leonard Online at
www.halleonard.com

The Muppet Show Theme

ABC-DEF-GHI

"C" Is for Cookie

Dream for Your Inspiration

Bein' Green

The First Time It Happens

Fraggle Rock Theme

Happiness Hotel

ABC-DEF-GHI

Words by JOE RAPOSO and JON STONE
Music by JOE RAPOSO

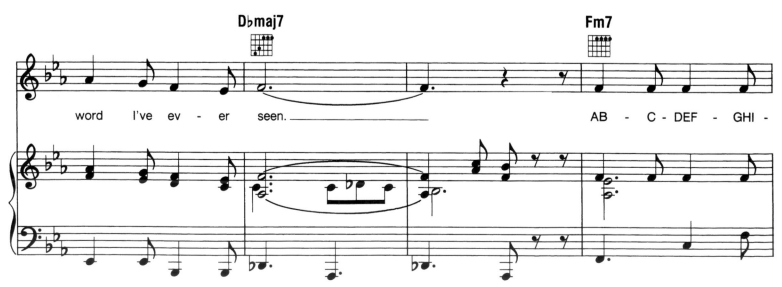

"C" IS FOR COOKIE

Words and Music by
JOE RAPOSO

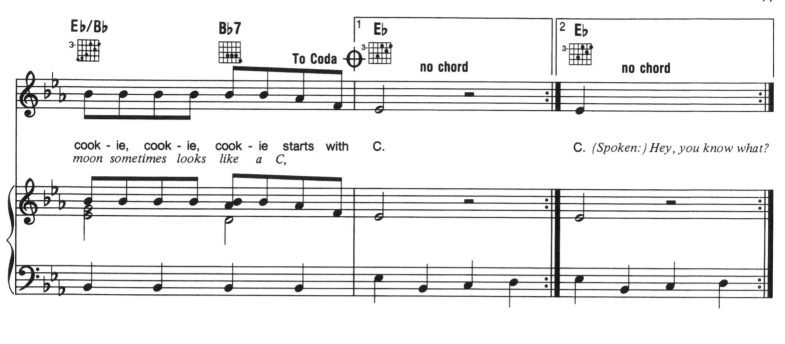

cook - ie, cook - ie, cook - ie starts with C.

moon sometimes looks like a C,

C. *(Spoken:) Hey, you know what?*

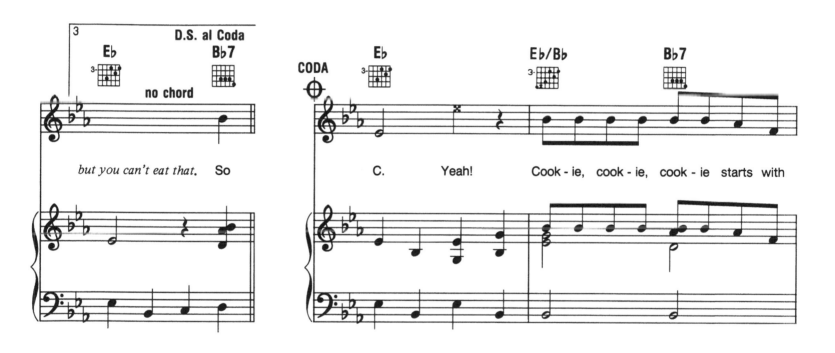

but you can't eat that. So

C. Yeah!

Cook - ie, cook - ie, cook - ie starts with

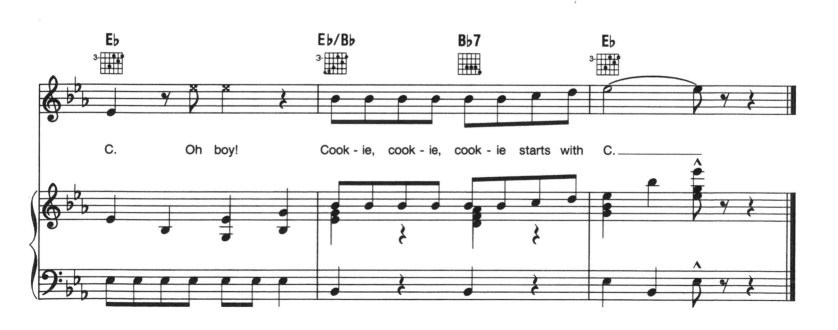

C. Oh boy!

Cook - ie, cook - ie, cook - ie starts with C.

THE MUPPET SHOW THEME

Words and Music by JIM HENSON
and SAM POTTLE

It's time to put on make - up. It's time to dress up right. __

It's time to raise the cur - tain on *The Mup - pet Show* __ to - night. To

in - tro - duce this rec - ord, that's what I'm here to do. __ So it

real - ly makes me hap - py to in - tro - duce __ to you

the first, original, genuine, no money back guarantee Muppet Show Cast Album!

DREAM FOR YOUR INSPIRATION

Words and Music by
SCOTT BROWNLEE

16

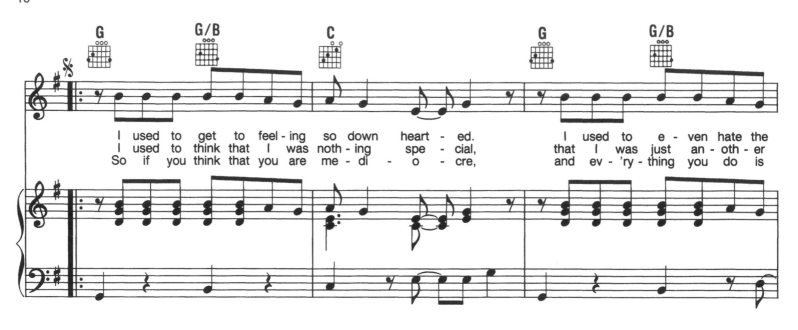

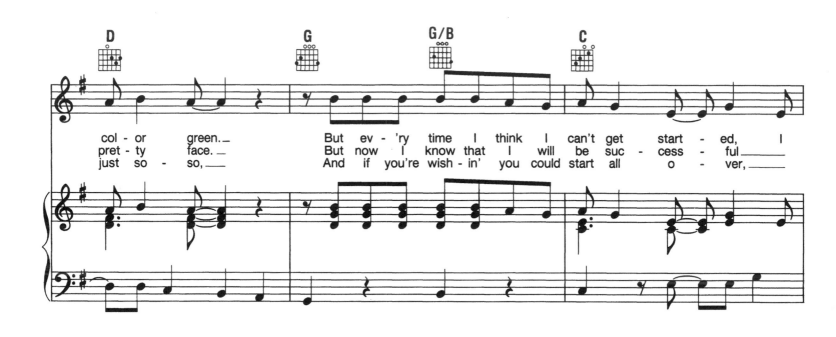

THE FIRST TIME IT HAPPENS

Words and Music by
JOE RAPOSO

22

FRAGGLE ROCK THEME

Words and Music by PHILIP BALSAM
and DENNIS LEE

1,3. Dance your cares a - way, — wor - ry's for an - oth - er day. —
2. Work your cares a - way, — danc - ing's for an - oth - er day. —

Let the mu - sic play — down at Frag - gle Rock.
Work your cares a - way —

Attention Doozers!

down at Frag - gle Rock.

down at Frag - gle Rock.

Hey look!   *There goes a Fraggle!*   *Come on, let's get outa here!*

3rd time - optional improvisation

Dance your cares_a-way, _ wor-ry's for an-oth-er day. _____ Let the mu - sic play. _

down at Frag - gle Rock.

down at Frag - gle Rock,

down at Frag - gle Rock,

down at Frag - gle Rock.

Down at Fraggle Rock.

BEIN' GREEN

Words and Music by
JOE RAPOSO

HAPPINESS HOTEL

Words and Music by
JOE RAPOSO

Bright Country Two

Oh, there's no fire ___ in the fire - place There's no car - pet on the floor Don't try to or - der din - ner there's no kitch - en an - y - more But if the road's been kind - a bump - y And you need to rest a

IT'S UP TO YOU

Words and Music by ALAN O'DAY
and JANIS LEIBHART

MAH-NÁ MAH-NÁ

By PIERO UMILIANI

MOVIN' RIGHT ALONG

Words and Music by PAUL WILLIAMS
and KENNETH L. ASCHER

47

MUPPET BABIES THEME

Words and Music by HANK SAROYAN
and ROB WALSH

Mup - pet Ba - bies, — we make our dreams_ come

true. _____ Mup - pet Ba - bies, — we'll

do the same_ for you. _____ When your room looks

THE RAINBOW CONNECTION

Words and Music by PAUL WILLIAMS
and KENNETH L. ASCHER

RUBBER DUCKIE

Words and Music by
JEFF MOSS

SAYING GOODBYE

Words and Music by
JEFF MOSS

Mah-Ná Mah-Ná

Movin' Right Along

Muppet Babies Theme

Rubber Duckie

Saying Goodbye